William Dalrymple

For the Use of Lord's Day Schools

Two scripture catechisms. I. For children who are just begun to read

distinctly. II. For those about eleven or twelve years of age

William Dalrymple

For the Use of Lord's Day Schools
*Two scripture catechisms. I. For children who are just begun to read distinctly. II.
For those about eleven or twelve years of age*

ISBN/EAN: 9783337172312

Printed in Europe, USA, Canada, Australia, Japan

Cover: Foto ©Lupo / pixelio.de

More available books at **www.hansebooks.com**

FOR THE

USE OF LORD'S DAY SCHOOLS,

TWO

SCRIPTURE CATECHISMS.

I.	II.
For Children who are just begun to read diftinctly ;	For thofe about eleven or twelve years of age ;

Both intended to prepare for the ufe of what is more
deeply Learned and Syftematical.

And thou fhalt teach them diligently unto thy children, and
fhalt talk of them when thou fitteft in thine houfe, and when thou
walkeft by the way, and when thou lieft down, and when thou rifeft
up, Deut. vi. 7. Compare Pfalm lxxviii. 5, 6, 7.

And that from a child thou haft known the *Holy Scriptures,*
which are able to make thee wife unto falvation, through Faith
which is in CHRIST JESUS, 2 Tim. iii. 15.

EDITION SECOND.

N. B. *The Firft Edition, confifting of more than a Thoufand Copies,
was bought up by the Inhabitants of the Town and Parifh of* AYR; *and
the greater part, by thofe of pious benevolence, to be given away.*

KILMARNOCK:

PRINTED BY J. WILSON,

For Meffrs. J. HUNTER and W. NEIL, Teachers of
the Englifh Schools in AYR.

M,DCC,LXXXVIII.

T. F. Torrance.

ABSTRACTING from confideration of all improvement, either when difcourfing myfelf, or hearing others upon great Subjects, I am beyond meafure delighted : but when I hear converfation of any other kind, efpecially the ufual difcourfe between you rich people, who are ftill contriving to heap up money, I feel a tediouſnefs in myfelf; and a concern for you, my Friends, who imagine you are employing your time to good purpofe, while you are only trifling. *Socrates in Plato.*

PREFACE.

THE human mind takes a tincture from objects with which it is at any time converfant. A ftrong one, from objects to which it is habituated, or with which it has been long converfant; but colours of the deepeft die, and moft durable, from objects with which it is furrounded at the time when itfelf is, next to void of all colour, and fufceptible of any; that is, the age of childhood. Whence it becometh of the utmoft confequence to familiarize them early with what is fair, comely, and beneficial. *Train up a child in the way wherein he fhould go*, Prov. xxii. 6. *and when he is old, he will not depart from it.* Science practical is then his proper bufinefs; or knowledge, which has a direct tendency to make him true, juft, compaffionate, and every way good: knowledge, in fhort, which conciliates *human nature* to the *divine*; and fits it, afterwards, for more clofe and direct methods of approach, by other kinds of ftudies. Compared with this, knowledge of things foreign to practice, or which do not readily admit of an obvious and ufeful application, is illiberal and fordid.

INSTRUCTION fhould be gradual, little in the beginning, a little and a little more as they advance; by

which method, the Reader or Hearer is put upon think-
ing for himfelf, and has his mind opened, too, by the
fame degrees. They who, at one leap, would gain fum-
mits of fcience and truth, will never benefit under the
wifeft Teachers; nor will the moft able Teachers be
fuccefsful, who aim at fo rapid an advance. Certain
neceffary fteps by this means are overlooked; or elfe the
whole becomes, in a very little time, infupportably bur-
denfome.

Conversation with youth who happen to have do-
cile tempers and fair minds, calls forth the latent feeds
of wifdom; and has the air of joint inquiry, when ma-
naged in an affable and familiar manner. Thus, the
curiofity and zeal of the mere ftranger is excited; that
of the difciple is encouraged; and, from one queftion
naturally arifing out of another, the mind is greatly
aided and forwarded in the purfuit of truth. Hence,
Solomon, as above, ufes the word *train*, or *catechife*, more
literally, as will be found in the margin. The great
Example of all Righteoufnefs, when he was only twelve
years of age, *was found in the Temple*, Luke ii. 46. *fit-
ting in the midft of the Doctors, both hearing them, and afking them Queftions*. An anecdote of fignal ufe, if pro-
perly attended to, for both parents and children.

Socrates' conftant rule, we are told, was, at the
time when any man was fpeaking, to give him his attention, efpecially if he thought him a wife man, or
much inclined to be fo; and, as one defirous to com-
prehend perfectly what he meant, to interrogate after-

wards, and fift him thoroughly concerning all that he had faid: to confider of it over and over again; and to compare his anfwers, in order to better mutual information. By this method, people of infignificance, and leaft worth the regarding, foon come to be difcovered. They are impatient of *Catechifing;* and, though not all at once to be given over, the trouble of *afking Queftions,* however pertinent, will not continue to be taken, even by the moft inclinable.

IGNORANCE, of courfe, muft take place. And this darkens the foul; as vice, it's moft ordinary offspring, doth diforder and debafe. By fuch, *Falfehood* is taken for *Truth,* and *Evil* for *Good.* They fancy *Truth and Good* to be where they are not; and thus erring from their right mark, every thing goes amifs. *Reafon* and *Paffion* are fet at variance. One paffion combats with another. The health of the foul is deftroyed. No lefs than complete wretchednefs doth follow. *The light of the body is the eye,* Matth. vi. 22, 23. *If, therefore, thine eye be fingle, thy whole body fhall be full of light. But, if thine eye be evil, thy whole body fhall be full of darknefs. If, therefore, the light that is in thee be darknefs, how great is that darknefs?*

IN healing this difeafe, by fetting the mind right, a greater fervice is done, than would be by healing any diftemper of the body. Yet how few think of it? In Religion, the cafe is alarming; for, if, by any means, a ferious turn come to be taken, owing to the want of foundation, unfteadinefs and ever-varying fentiments

muſt obtain. They are driven *to and fro*, backward and forward continually. They are *children*, when they ſhould be *men;* and *liable to be toſſed by every wind of doctrine, and cunning craftineſs of thoſe who lie in wait to deceive*, Eph. iv. 14. Says a great writer, * " Imagina-
" tion operates without control, when it is not checked
" with knowledge; the ignorant, at the ſame time, are
" delighted with wonder: and the more wonderful a
" ſtory is, the more welcome it is made." He adds,
" this may ſerve as an apology for ancient Writers,
" even when they relate and believe facts to us incre-
" dible." A like apology may be made for believing doctrines, however incredible, when dictated with art, and a vociferous manner.

SCIENCE lies latent, till excited and brought to light by fair, diligent, and deep inquiry; and they who are not aſhamed to learn, but who, with *meekneſs and fear*, aſk ſuitable queſtions, poſſeſs an admirable quality. Of all others, they are ſafeſt from the above fatal conſe-quences of ignorance and error. They are not apt to be entangled by cunning fallacies, and ſly evaſions.

SPEECHES and Lectures, when long, are eaſily forgot; and ſerve not ſo effectually the end, as by unaſſuming converſe. Whilſt the one is calculated to *entertain*, the other *holds faſt*, and becomes the foundation of *ſettled o-pinion*. Human authority, in correſpondence with the divine Rule, ſecures effect for the moſt god-like ends.

* Lord Kaimes' Sketches of the Hiſtory of Man, B. 1. Sk. 1.

No judicious perfon, therefore, will find fault with joining two plain *Scripture Catechifms* with the excellent views of thofe who did recommend the *Shorter and Larger Ones* more generally ufed in Scotland, for the benefit of Church Members: and to which, vaft multitudes, when come to years, have been greatly indebted.

For one who has had long experience, the defire of keeping up a rehearfal from thofe moft accurate fyftems can never be blamed; but the contrary. A judgement of difcretion, both among Minifters and Teachers of Youth in fchools, may be proper as to abridging certain of the anfwers, which, in their defign, may be, notwithftanding, quite complete. More advanced years will find little or no difficulty to become mafter of the whole. Till that happen, the profitable, or what conduces to produce moft good, fhould meet with no blame. Without being arrogant, one may prefume, that a purpofe fo beneficial, unlefs *fingularly defective*, fhould be encouraged. And, if *defective*, why not give room to others of equally generous views, and with better abilities? Let this be underftood, and duly weighed, in the fight of an all-knowing and impartial Judge. The facrednefs of *Truth* will never fuffer any to oppofe the man, who has the fuccefs of it obvioufly upon his heart.

He who intends the beft benefit of thofe whom he endeavours to inftruct, ought to have fome knowledge of human nature; and the various capacities, as well as difpofitions of his pupils. Nor ought he to forget *the words of him who said,* in support of a willing, though perhaps comparatively deficient actor, *he who is not a-gainst me, is for me.* *He who is not with me* at all, and yet obstructs a sincere and cordial designer, *is against me.* Blind positiveness banishes afar both reason and truth. Random speeches, or readily deciding on points not thoroughly sifted, are no more to be allowed, than talking of things whereof we are ignorant, as if we knew them. It is not what a man *wills* only, but what he *can,* that entitles him to cavil, or reproach. Parts may appear weak, or reprehensible, which, to a mind comprehending the whole, are not so devoid of usefulness, and even beauty or grace.

ANNEXED to the love of excellence, is the desire of generating, or stamping upon other minds, some like thoughts; and should his power attain so high, of raising up and nurturing an intellectual progeny of godly, generous sentiments and fair ideas. When the soul is thus endowed, it cannot be unmindful of *Him who hath made us to be partakers of the inheritance of the Saints in light; who hath delivered us from the power of darkness, and hath translated us into the kingdom of his dear Son: in whom we have redemption through his blood, even the forgiveness of sins; who is the image of the invisible God, the first born, chief or head of every creature; the first-born from the dead, that in all things he might have the pre-eminence,* Col. i. 12, *&c.* Love of beauty so glorious, so consummate, seizes the pious breast; and inclines him to be distinguished, if it were only among *babes,* whose conceptions at the time are low, but will not always be fixed to what is inferior.

Even among the wife ancients, meetings were deemed things folemn and important; efpecially thofe for the
purpofe of *Converfation:* becaufe in thefe, above every
other, ought to appear the effential character of man, as
a rational and focial being. May *Chriftian Parents,*
and even *Houfeholders* without children, apply this to
their frequent opportunities at home; and it is odds, but
they improve, or ftand convicted. As they go along
through life, and when they have moft leifure, with
the cleareft call of Providence, they will furely ftop
from their ordinary employments, and grace the *Lord's
Days Evenings,* with holding out to the neareft objects
of their affection, the *rich paternity* of him *who fo loved
the world, as to give his only begotten Son, that whofoever
believeth on him fhould not perifh, but have everlafting life,*
John iii. 16. *This, this is the work of God,* chap. vi. 29.

A RETURN of gratitude will make even of a *daftard* an
enthufiaft; and difclofe him, in the end, to be born with a
difpofition the moft excellent; or *begotten to it, by the word
of truth, which liveth and abideth,* in the effects of it, *for e-
ver.* Love of this fort muft endure, being united to that
which is eternal. *Covet earneftly the beft gifts. Strive to
excell* in them. But *having a more excellent way* fhewed
us, and more in every one's power, let pure, fpiritual affection for kindred fouls never fail. Every fpecies of
impiety is the ufual confequence of not attending to this.

AND fhould it feem to attract obfervation, with un-
fuitable remarks, contraft thefe with this, that, as without the fenfe of *fhame* attending bafe conduct, fo, with-

B

out the fenſe of *honour* in doing what is honourable, neither communities, nor private perſons, can execute
what is noble. Moreover, *Bleſſed are ye when men ſhall
revile you, and perſecute you, and ſpeak all manner of evil
againſt you falſely for* CHRIST's *ſake. Rejoice and be exceeding glad, for great is your reward in Heaven,* Matth.
v. 11, 12. *Then ſhall the righteous ſhine forth as the ſun, in
the kingdom of their Father,* Matth. xiii. 43. *And they who
turn many unto righteouſneſs, as the ſtars for ever and ever,*
Dan. xii. 3. *Who hath ears to hear, let him hear.*

EXAMPLES ſtriking ſhould be produced at firſt, or
when your *multiplied ſelves* are ſetting out, when attention is moſt awake ; and, being ſtrongly imprinted
on the mind, they may eaſily occur afterwards. That
of CHRIST requires no nice and delicate ſelection from
it ; *for he did all things well.* When occaſions offer to
recollect theſe, there can be no want, as to particulars,
leſs danger of erring ; and, after proper *Catechetical inſtruction* by tender love, not ſo much difficulty as in for-
getting the diſtreſs of piouſly meant, but extreme hard-
ſhips to *memorial exerciſe* upon what neither was, nor
could be comprehended at the time. The young are
curious, in proportion to the vigour of their faculties ;
and it ſhould be the delight of mature age, to commu-
nicate, to beget and cheriſh the ideas of uſeful knowledge, to immortalize them : for the ſake of which, a-
bove every other, love to offspring is ſtrong. *If we
know theſe things, happy are we, if we do them. Amen.*

CATECHISM I.

Q. 1. **W**HO *is the* SAVIOUR *of the world?*

A. JESUS CHRIST.

Q. 2. *Why is he called* JESUS?

A. Becaufe he faves his people from their fins, Matth. i. 21.

ADVICE TO CATECHIST.

Make the child, or children, read that laft paffage.

Q. 3. *And why is he called* CHRIST?

A. Becaufe that word fignifies *anointed;* and he was anointed with the HOLY GHOST, which is the *power of God,* Acts x. 38. Read.

Q. 4. *Has he any other name given him in Scripture?*

A. He is likewife ftyled LORD, or MAS-TER, John xiii. 13. Read.

Q. 5. *Who was his Mother?*
A. The *Virgin Mary.*

C A T E C H I S T.

Let children fee the Hiftory of this, Luke i. chap. from verfe 26.

Q. 6. *Where was he born?*
A. In *Bethlehem* of *Judea.*

C A T E C H I S T.

Let them fee and read the hiftory of this, Luke ii. from the beginning.

Q. 7. *In what ftate or condition was he born?*
A. In a low, or poor ftate.

C A T E C H I S T.

The above paffages may be read two or three times during the currency of the week; to fix upon their memories each of the texts, and their proper fenfe.

Q. 8. *How long did he live with* Mary, *before he began to preach publicly?*
A. About thirty years, Luke iii. 23.
Q. 9. *Who was his Forerunner?*
A. *John*, called the *Baptift*, Luke i. 76.
Q. 10. *How did* John *prepare his way?*
A. By exhorting men to repent; and baptizing thofe with water, who confeffed their fins, Matth. iii. 1—7.

C A T E C H I S T.

Tell the children, as they read this paffage, that

a *Prophet* is one whom God enables to know things long before they happen. That *Isaiah*, in particular, lived near 700 years before CHRIST was born. That *Jerusalem* was the greatest city in all *Judea*. That *Judea* was a country, and *Jordan* a river. In requiring an answer, afterwards, to each of these, let the children be allowed to speak their own language, and insist not for the precise words as they are printed.

Q. 11. *Was* JESUS *himself baptized?*
A. Yes; that he might be an example of all righteousness, Matth. iii. 13, to the end.

CATECHIST.

Tell the children, CHRIST had no sin to repent of, or confess; but, by submitting to be baptized, he owned *John* publicly to be a *Prophet*.

Q. 12. *What happened to him after his baptism?*
A. The *Spirit of God* came down from Heaven upon him.

CATECHIST.

Tell them, that the *Spirit of God*, and *Holy Ghost*, or *Power of the Highest*, are the same; as in Quest. 3.

Q. 13. *Did he then immediately enter upon his office of preaching the Gospel publicly?*
A. Not till he had gone through a great and remarkable trial. To be seen, and carefully read, out of Matth. iv. 1—12.

CATECHIST.

Upon the nature of the different temptations, as yet, little must be said; unless, that the *devil* can do nothing, without allowance from GOD; and that, as long as people are good, they have nothing to fear from him. He would have had CHRIST employ the power of GOD, which came down from Heaven upon him, to eafe his hunger; to make a great and proud fhew with, before all the people, when they went into the Temple or Church; and laft of all, to ferve bad ends. But CHRIST would not yield to him, no not for a moment; and, by a right ufe of the *Scripture*, he completely conquered him. Talk of thefe things to them, in a plain agreeable way.

Q. 14. *How many* Difciples *did* CHRIST *choofe to be generally with him?*

A. Twelve, whom he named *Apoftles.*

CATECHIST.

Tell the children, that the word *difciple* fignifies a fcholar. That CHRIST has many fuch *difciples* or fcholars. And that the word *apoftle* fignifies a meffenger. That the Twelve were fent firft with the meffage of *Chrift's Religion*, to all the people of *Judea;* and afterwards to the people of the *whole earth.* Their firft meffage may be feen, and read, out of Matth. x. from the beginning; and the laft meffage, out of Matth. xxviii. from verfe 18.

Q. 15. *What do you mean by* CHRIST'S *religion?*

A. The *good things* which he would have all his *Difciples* or *Scholars* to do.

Q. 16. *Can you tell me fome of the chief of thofe* good things?

A. Yes; That they who had been bad before, fhould be fo no more; but learn to do well: likewife pray to GOD, read his word, and give thanks to him.

CATECHIST.

Let them know, that the firſt of the above is the ſame with *repenting*. Tell how much they are obliged to ALMIGHTY GOD for their life, meat, drink, friends, &c. Alſo, that they ſhould love him, and all their neighbours. How good the *Heavenly Father* is ; and what a pleaſant way of living, to be quiet and peaceable, not eaſily put into anger, and never to give bad names, far leſs ſtrike.

Q. 17. *What did* CHRIST *do, to confirm this wiſe and uſeful teaching?*

A. He gave ſight to the blind, hearing to the deaf, ſpeech to the dumb, ſoundneſs and ſtrength to the lame, and even life to the dead.

CATECHIST.

If this anſwer be too long, or indeed any of the above, they may be eaſily broken thus; What did CHRIST do for the blind? He gave them ſight. What for the deaf? &c. &c.

Q. 18. *How are theſe great works named in Scripture?*

A. Miracles.

CATECHIST.

Let the children read, for illuſtrating theſe, Luke vii. from verſe 11. Explain the words *widow, compaſſion, bier* or coffin, *glorifying* or praiſing, *rumour, region* or country, *diſciples of John,* why called *Baptiſt, goſpel,* an old word for good news, or glad-tidings.

Q. 19. *Were the labours of thoſe few men ſucceſsful, in ſo great and difficult an employment?*

A. Yes; great multitudes believed the *Gospel*, and were baptized, both men and women.

CATECHIST.

Let the children read Matth. iv. from verse 23. to the end. Tell them that *Syria* was a country. That *people possessed with devils* were not to be cured, but by a power from God. That *lunatics* signify such as are mad. And that the *palsy* takes away the use, and sometimes the feeling, of hands, feet, tongue, and whole body. To understand something of the great numbers who followed Christ and his Apostles, they may also read how many were fed by him at one time, out of Matth. xiv. 8, &c. See now, if they mind the word *Disciples*, or scholars. Compare with this John vi. 5——15. Observe to them, what a kind heart Christ has; that *fragments* are the small broken pieces of meat; and that it is a great wrong to throw them away, when so many poor folk would be glad of them.

Q. 20. *Did* CHRIST *declare to all men their duty?*

A. Yes.

Q. 21. *Did he likewise correct their vices freely?*

A. Yes.

CATECHIST.

Here let the children read Mark viii. 14——22. with Matth. 23. from verse 13. Tell them of the use of *leaven* among flour, or meal. That the *Pharisees* were great hypocrites, and spread their bad opinions and manners, like *leaven*, among the poor weak people; as did the flatterers of *Herod*, who was a very bad king. That the *Scribes* were men who pretended to have skill in Religion above all others; and, with the base hypocritical *Pharifees*, were beloved by the multitude. Explain the examples there given of their vile falfehood; at leaft fome of the eafieft to be underftood, fo far as verfe 13.

Q. 22. *How did the* Scribes *and* Pharifees *bear to be fpoken to fo honeftly and boldly?*

A. They were much provoked; and, at length, did contrive how they might put him to death.

Q. 23. *Did they ever get this horrid defign brought about?*

A. Yes; God allowed them, to fhew what great fufferings his beloved Son could bear, in defence of truth; to confirm all his holy Rules, and moft precious Promifes; and to be an example of patience to his Followers, in every future age of the Church. See John xviii. 37.

C A T E C H I S T.

Tell them how dear to God *truth* is; and how neceffary to mankind. That to fuffer for it, is the nobleft degree of goodnefs, if people do not complain; and that this is true *patience*.

Q. 24. *By what means did they bring about the death of* Christ?

A. They prevailed upon one of his *Difciples*, by an offer of money, to betray him into their hands.

C A T E C H I S T.

Let the children read this melancholy hiftory out of

Mark xiv. 43—46. compared with Matth. xxvi.
14—16. See if they underſtand what *one of the twelve*
means.   Let them know of *Judas'* other name *Iſca-*
riot, to diſtinguiſh him from another Apoſtle of the
ſame name, who was the brother of *James*.   Explain
the ſad guilt of betraying a friend into trouble, by ap-
pearing to love him; and the ſign of great love, which
he then put on.

Q. 25. *Could* Christ, *if he had choſen,*
have got away from them?

A. Very eaſily.

C A T E C H I S T.

To prove this, let them read the noble account in
John xviii. 1——10. Explain the *brook Cedron*, as ly-
ing between two high hills, covered each with trees
and bruſhwood.   Therefore, though it was moon-light,
they needed *lanthorns* and *torches;* which may eaſily
be diſtinguiſhed.   Christ's enemies fell to the ground;
and, when he allowed them to riſe, he would not ſuf-
fer them to touch him, till he had obtained leave, and
ſufficient time for his weak and frighted *Apoſtles to go*
their way.   Jesus knew what *Judas* was carrying on;
and choſe this private place, not for ſafety, but to me-
ditate and pray.

Q. 26. *What was the nature of that death*
which Christ *ſuffered?*

A. It is called *Crucifixion*, or nailing to a
Croſs.

Q. 27. *What like was the ſhape of the*
Croſs?

A. Like the large letter T; and to the
upper part, the hands were nailed; as both
feet, put together, were nailed to the long-

eſt; and then, the whole wooden Croſs was raiſed up, and the ſmalleſt end of it fixed in the ground.

Q. 28. *Muſt not this have been very pain-ful?*

A. Exceedingly ſo; becauſe, beſides the weight of a whole body thus hung, it was deemed a curſe, and done only to the meaneſt and worſt of men.

CATECHIST.

Let the children know how full of little bones and ſinews, both hands and feet are; that the tearing of theſe aſunder, produces the moſt exquiſite torture; that the blood, being confined by the large nails, could only drop; and that, owing to this, the life was long kept in; ſometimes for whole days and nights together, till hunger and thirſt, as well as pain, did put an end to it.

Q. 29. *What became of* CHRIST's *body, after he died?*

A. He was buried in a new grave, or ſe-pulchre.

CATECHIST.

Let the children read this twice or thrice over from Matth. xxvii. 57——62. *Arimathea* was either the city of *Joſeph's* birth, or common reſidence; though, as a *Counſellor*, or great *Magiſtrate*, he behoved ſometimes to live in *Jeruſalem*. *Pilate* was the chief governor of all *Judea*; but appointed to this high office, by *Auguſtus Cæſar*, the emperor of *Rome*. *Sepulchres*, in that country, were hewed out of ſolid rock; and either covered with a large ſtone, or ſhut up at the mouth by one, in the manner of a door. The *Jews* were often at great expence in burying their dead bodies, by taking out the bowels, and filling in rich spices, and gums, to keep them from rotting ; at least for a long time. Let them read John xix. 38, to the end. Their gardens were their common burial-places, or without cities ; a much wiser method than ours.

Q. 30. *Did he continue in that grave, sepulchre, or tomb ?*

A. No. He arose again, on the third day after his death.

CATECHIST.

Let them read Matth. xxviii. 1——9. But questions upon this to be delayed for another exercise.

Q. 31. *Of whom was he seen after his resurrection ?*

A. Of his Apostles, and several others.

CATECHIST.

Let them read the xx. and xxi. chapters of *John ;* and the fine story of the two Disciples going to *Emmaus,* Luke xxiv. verse 13, *&c.*

Q. 32. *Was he seen by his followers at leisure, and more than once ?*

A. Yes. From the passages formerly read, it appears that they did eat and drink with, and that they were allowed to touch, yea to handle him.

CATECHIST.

Here the children should read Acts i. 1, 2, 3.

Obferve to them, that *Acts* fignify doings. That *Luke*, who wrote the gofpel, did alfo write the *Acts*, or doings of *the Apoftles*. *Infallible proofs*, or figns, were fuch as could not be miftaken. *The kingdom of God* on earth, is, his Gofpel; and prepares men for the more glorious *kingdom of God* in Heaven.

Q. 33. *For how long a time did he appear to, and converfe with his Difciples?*

A. For the fpace of forty days. Read again, Acts i. 2, and 3. verfes.

Q. 34. *Of what things did he chiefly dif-courfe with his* Apoftles *all that time?*

A. Chiefly of the work in which they were to be employed, after he fhould go to Heaven; and the affiftances of the *Holy Ghoft*, which he would fend down upon them, from thence. Read Acts i. 4.

Q. 35. *How was the* Holy Ghoft, *or mighty power of* GOD, *to affift them?*

A. Firft, by bringing all things he had before fpoken, to their remembrance, John xvi. 12—14. And then, fecondly, by enabl-ing them, from that time forward, to fpeak every kind of language.

CATECHIST.

Here caufe them read with leifure and attention, the hiftory of that matter in Acts ii. 1———14. Why *cloven?* Becaufe Tongues were various. Why *fiery?* Be-caufe the effects were moft powerful. The *noife* ferv-ed only to awaken their notice.

Q. 36. *Were the endeavours of thofe few men*

C

successful in so extensive and difficult an employment ?

A. Yes; great multitudes received the word, and were baptized, both men and women.

C A T E C H I S T.

Here should be read, with great care and seriousness, Acts ii. verse 41, to the end. Let the children know, from thence. how lovely, both in their tempers and lives, the earliest converts to the Gospel were. They were often in religious converse, or *fellowship* together. They *prayed* much at home, and attended Public Worship. They frequently met to *break bread* in the *Lord's Supper*, agreeable to Matth. xxvi. 26, 27. They were chearful, contented, and *charitable* to one another. To prove all which yet farther, read Acts iv. verse 31, to the end.

Q. 37. *Did the* Jews *forsake their old law of Rites and Ceremonies, to embrace the pure spiritual doctrine of* CHRIST ?

A. Yes; even many of the *priests* themselves *became obedient to the Faith,* Acts vi. 7. That is, to the rules of the gospel.

Q. 38. *And were the* gentiles, *or heathens, brought off from the worship of their* false gods ?

A. Yes, in vast multitudes; so that, very soon, the *Christian Religion* prevailed throughout most of the known and civilized nations of the world.

Q. 39. *What became of these converts to the* Christian Religion ?

A. They formed themfelves into religious Societies, or *Churches*.

Q. 40. *And what were their employments,
when they met ?*

A. It was to pray, praife, difcourfe pi-
oufly, hear the *word of God ;* and to cele-
brate, as before faid, the *Lord's Supper*, by
eating bread, and drinking wine, in remembrance of CHRIST's broken body and
fhed blood.

Q. 41. *Upon what day of the week did they
obferve their ordinary religious meetings ?*

A. On the *firft day of the week*, called the
Lord's Day, in commemoration of his tri-
umphant refurrection from the dead, 1 Cor.
xvi. 2. Rev. i. 10.

Q. 42. *Who were appointed to direct, or fu-
perintend, in thofe religious meetings ?*

A. Men of moft improved integrity, and
capacity ; named fometimes *Bifhops*, at o-
ther times *Elders, Paftors* and *Teachers*.

Q. 43. *And upon whom was the chief care of
the poor devolved ?*

A. Upon fober and well known liberal
men, called, from their office, *Deacons*, or
miniftering fervants.

END OF CATECHISM I.

C A T E C H I S M   II.

Q. 1. TO *whom was the* Virgin Mary *ef-poufed?*
A. To a man in low circumftances, whofe name was *Jofeph.*

Q. 2. *From what family were* Jofeph *and* Mary *defcended, or come of?*
A. From the family of *David*, who, many hundred years before this time, had been king of Ifrael.

C A T E C H I S T.

Ifrael fignifies the fame with *Jews;* becaufe old *Jacob,* the grandfon of *Abraham,* and who likewife was named *Ifrael,* was the father of twelve fons, who were heads of the *twelve Tribes.* And the whole are called *Jews,* from the land of *Judea,* in which they dwelt.

Q. 3. *Who was king of* Judea, *when our blessed* LORD *was born?*

A. *Herod*, a very wicked man, and not a *Jew* by birth.

CATECHIST.

Put the children in mind of his murdering both wives and sons; partly from a cruel disposition, and partly from suspecting them to have too much the love of his subjects.

Q. 4. *Were* Herod *and the* Jews, *at this time, under the power of any other emperor or king?*

A. They were governed, in a good measure, by *Augustus Cæsar*, the Roman emperor, then, the very greatest in the whole world.

Q. 5. *How do you know this?*

A. *Augustus* ordered all the inhabitants of *Judea* to be taxed; that is, to pay money every year as they were able. Read Luke ii. 1, 2.

Q. 6. *When was* JESUS CHRIST *born?*

A. At the very time when the names of the *Jewish people* were enrolled, or taken down in a book; and the sums of money likewise made mention of, that every person after that should be obliged to pay. Read the above Luke ii. verse 3.

Q. 7. *Was the birth of* JESUS *attended with any thing extraordinary?*

A. The *Angel of the Lord* appeared in the

C 3

night, to fome humble and induftrious fhepherds, not far from *Bethlehem*, and fpoke of it to them. Read again the laft cited chapter of Luke, from verfe 8.

CATECHIST.

The *Angels of the Lord* are Spirits, who, for the good of men, were fometimes allowed to appear to them in their own form ; and, at other times, with a *glory* or light around them, as here. They are very powerful, and very good; fee Pfalm ciii. 20, 21. We become like them, when we are diligent in GOD's fervice ; fee and keep this in mind, when you pray, as in Matth. vi. 10. *Thy will be done in earth, as it is in heaven.* If we obey like them, we fhall, in another world, go to them, and be equal with them. See Matth. xxii. 30. *For in the refurrection*, or future ftate, *they neither marry, nor are given in marriage ; but are as the Angels of* GOD *in Heaven.*

Q. 8. *Was the birth of* JESUS *followed with any thing extraordinary ?*

A: Yes; upon his being prefented in the Temple, according to the cuftom of the *Jews*, a venerable old man, whofe name was *Simeon*, took him in his arms, and faid great things concerning him ; as did, likewife, *Anna a Prophetefs.* Read both thefe fine accounts ftill, in the fame fecond of *Luke*, from verfe 22, to verfe 29.

CATECHIST.

The days of purification were days for women in child-bed to be kept very quiet, left their health fhould fuffer. Their firft vifit was, to the *Houfe of God.* A

Lamb was an offering for rich people; and the poor-er fort were as acceptable with their low-priced pair of *Turtle doves.* *Joseph and Mary*, no doubt, would give the best they were able to afford. They must, there-fore, have been *poor*; and *poverty* is no mark of GOD's dislike. *Simeon* was just in his dealing with men; and a regular *devout* worshipper of GOD. The *consolation*, or comfort *of Israel*, which he expected, and *waited for*, was CHRIST the *Saviour*, The *Holy Ghost*, or wisdom of GOD, was upon him; and, by this means, he fore-told what sort of *Saviour* CHRIST would prove. *Sal-vation*, in verse 30th, is put for him who should bring it to pass. *Light* is knowledge. The *Gentiles* were i-dolatrous heathens. It was the *glory*, or *praise of If-rael*, that CHRIST was come of them, and to preach to them in person. *All people*, both *Jews* and *Heathens*, were to be saved by him. The *Jews*, who did not believe, grew every day worse, or *fell*. They who did believe, *rose again* to become good and happy. O what a *heart-piercing sword* would it be to *Mary*, to fee her excellent and most dear Son hanging upon the Cross!

Night and day signify only very often; or *morn and even prayers*, which no good young person should ne-glect: least of all, people who are grown up. This is a great ease to an afflicted, or *widowed* soul. *Re-demption* is deliverance; and the greatest of all deliver-ance is, from sin and misery.

Another extraordinary thing which followed JESUS' birth, was, the visit of the three wife men from the East. Read the whole second Chapter of Matthew.

These wise men were well acquainted with the places and motions of the *heavenly bodies*; and they were rich, as appears from the presents made by them to *Joseph* and *Mary*. They discovered a new *star*, and of an uncommon largeness and beauty. But, with-

out more help than what was merely human, they
could not have underſtood the deſign of it. At this
time, throughout all the Eaſt, a great king was expected; as both Jewiſh and heathen hiſtorians do witneſs. The prophecies of the old Teſtament might
lead to this; and ALMIGHTY GOD might intimate to
thoſe great Scholars, that he was now born; and,
that the ſtar would point him out. They, therefore,
ſought very early to make friends with him. At firſt,
the *ſtar* ſtood over *Jeruſalem;* and brought the *wiſe
men* thither. This alarmed *Herod's* cruel jealouſy;
and troubled all the inhabitants of *Jeruſalem*, leſt, as
did happen, he ſhould ſhed much innocent blood.

Obſerve *Herod's* cunning, as well as his cruelty, in
gathering the chief Prieſts together, on a pretence of
religion. Likewiſe, the clearneſs of ancient propheſy,
as to the place of CHRIST's birth. Then, admire *Providence*, firſt, in preventing the murder of the LORD
JESUS; and next, in providing ſuch a ſeaſonable and
neceſſary ſupply of money, to carry *Joſeph, Mary,* and
the *bleſſed Infant* down to *Egypt;* and to maintain
them there, till *Herod* ſhould die. None but a *Herod*
could kill ſo many poor babes, and make ſo many ten-
der-hearted fathers and mothers miſerable. Let the
Catechumens be directed to think of *Rachel weeping for
her children.* This *Rachel* was old *Jacob's* favourite
wife, who was dead more than two thouſand years:
but ſhe had been buried near to *Bethlehem;* and *Saint
Matthew*, to expreſs the deepeſt motherly ſorrow,
ſpeaks of the reſt under her name, as did the *prophet
Jeremiah* before him, chap. xxxi-15. becauſe ſhe was
one of very ſtrong natural affections. Both of them
would ſeem to ſay, that ſo horrible a ſpilling of infant-
blood, was enough, as it were, to move the dead them-
ſelves.

Let this ſad ſtory teach every young ſoul to beware
of cruelty. If *Herod* had not begun early, and with
ſmaller inſtances, he would not have murdered; but,

having once begun, he could eafily go on. Perhaps from killing flies, and torturing dogs and cats, he did fo harden his nature, as to kill and torture any thing. A good natured heathen faid, *It was better to be Herod's hog, than his child.* Tell the reafon of this, from fwine's flefh being prohibited to the *Jews.*

Q. 9. *What came of* Jofeph, Mary, *and the* bleffed Infant, *after* Herod's *death?*

A. They returned to the land of *Judea,* and abode in one of the moft retired parts of it, named *Galilee;* and where was the low and much defpifed town of *Nazareth.*

Q. 10. *Who, at the time of their return, reigned in* Herod's *ftead?*

A. A fon of his, named *Archelaus.*

Q. 11. *Is there any thing taken notice of in the* New Teftament, *concerning the early part of* CHRIST's *life?*

A. At the age of twelve years, he went up to *Jerufalem,* and gave very public proofs of uncommon knowledge.

CATECHIST.

Let pupils read this hiftory in Luke ii. from verfe 41. and obferve to them, firft, that though the *parents* of JESUS are fpoken of, yet had he no earthly father; and therefore, he is called the *Son of God.* The world for a good while, however, knew not of this. He was underftood, by the *Jews,* to be *Jofeph's* fon, as well as *Mary's.* And becaufe *Mary* was his undoubted mother; therefore, in great modefty, he ofteneft fpeaks of himfelf as the *Son of Man.* Secondly, obferve what the *Paffover feaft* was inftituted in remembrance of. Third, the great piety of *Jofeph and Mary.* Fourth, what an early example of the fame thing our *divine*

Saviour was. Fifth, that his religion was founded in distinct knowledge. Sixth, that he gave his countenance and approbation to the useful work of catechizing youth. Seventh, how tender and mild his mother *Mary* was. She does not complain of what she thought a wrong thing, in rash and harsh words. Eight, the suitableness of CHRIST's reply: he had come to the *feast;* and would willingly see all the days of it out. Ninthly, his amiable pattern of *subjection.* And, in the last place, by the *increase of wisdom* which he shewed, along with *bodily stature,* how much giving evidence of the same thing is bound upon others; and how much this doth please GOD certainly, and, for most part also, please men.

Q. 12. *How long did* JESUS *continue with his parent, or parents?*

A. Till he was about thirty years of age; and till *John Baptist* had fully prepared his way.

CATECHIST.

We read not of *Joseph* at this time; and therefore presume that he was dead.

Q. 13. *Whose son was* John?

A. The son of *Zacharias,* a Jewish priest, by his wife *Elizabeth.*

CATECHIST.

Read the remarkable history of his conception and birth, Luke i. from verse 5, to the end of verse 25. This happened in the days of the very wicked *Herod.* There were many priests, at that time, who had different employments; and many who were employed the same way, had their different *courses,* or turns. Each of which were named from their principal family. *In-*

cen/e has a fweet fmell; and was, therefore, ufed in time of *prayer*, to let the people know, how acceptable this duty was to ALMIGHTY GOD. Though *John's*-parents were both good, yet they were tried with the want of children, for moſt part of their life. Into the Temple of GOD, no other than a *good Angel* could be allowed to come; and Zacharias, who was a *prieſt*, or *miniſter*, fhould have known this. What he fuffer-ed, however, for not believing, made the unexpected birth of his fon better known.

Q. 14. *To whom did* John *preach?*

A. To the *Jews*.

Q. 15. *How much older was he than* CHRIST?

A. Only ſix months; as appears from *Luke's* hiſtory, chap. i. verſe 26, read to verſe 57.

CATECHIST.

Efpoufed, or contracted. *Houfe*, or family. JESUS, or SAVIOUR. *Reign* ſpiritual, and not temporal, or worldly, fuch as the *Jews* wifhed. The word *called* is very often put for the very thing itſelf which is fpok-en of; witnefs, Matth. v. 9, 19. 1 John iii. 1. CHRIST reigns in Heaven, by the appointment of his *Father*, over angels, as well as men. *Holy Ghoſt*, or power of the Higheſt. What a modeſt, pious, and believing wo-man was *Mary?*

Q. 16. *Did* John *make known to the* Jews *the coming of our Saviour?*

A. He did; and that the *kingdom of God*, to be begun and carried on by him, was at hand.

C A T E C H I S T.

Read this, Matth. iii. from verfe 1. Called *the king-dom of God*, becaufe the greateft that ever was, or fhall be upon earth; and becaufe it was foretold feveral hundred years before this, by this name. See Dan. vii. 13, 14. *Ancient of Days*, the Eternal, Almighty GOD. *Son of Man*, CHRIST.

Q. 17. *What errors and fins were the* Jews, *at that time, moft commonly addicted to?*

A. They trufted to their various nation-al religious privileges; to the outward forms of worfhip; and to their being de-fcended from *Abraham*, the friend of GOD.

C A T E C H I S T.

Read the laft cited iii. chap. of Matth. from verfe 7. The *Pharifees* were grofs hypocrites. The *Sadducees* did not believe another world, after death. They hated one another, and confirmed one another in their fatal errors.

Q. 18. *What did* John *do, to correct thefe fatal errors and crimes?*

A. He taught in very plain terms the ne-ceffity of *good works;* and that, without thefe, they could not go to Heaven. *Fruits* fignify works.

Q. 19. *Did many of the* Jews *believe him to be a true prophet?*

A. They did, and were baptized of him, confefling their fins.

CATECHIST.

Read John v. 33, 35. *Light*, preacher. *Shining*, clear and intelligible. *Burning*, powerful and efficacious.

Q. 20. *Was* JESUS *among the number of those who were baptized?*

A. He was, though free from all sin, that he might bear witness to *John*.

Q. 21. *Who was Emperor of* Rome, *when* John *began to preach?*

A. Tiberius Cæsar.

CATECHIST.

Read Luke iii. 1. and obferve, firſt, that the word *Tetrarch* ſignifies one who governed a fourth part. *Pontius Pilate*, who was an idolatrous heathen, had the beſt *fourth* of the whole. The *Tetrarch* of *Galilee* was cruel *Herod's* ſon; and, in many reſpects, was too like him.

Here the *Catechumens* may be made acquainted with that wonderful prophecy about CHRIST, in Gen. xlix. 10. They know who *Jacob* was; likewiſe, that each of his children were heads of a *Jewiſh Tribe*. That of *Judah* was to produce Kings, and other chief Magiſtrates, till *Shiloh* came. That is CHRIST MESSIAH, or the great perſon to be ſent, as the word *Shiloh* ſignifies. *And to him the gathering of the* heathen *nations* was to be. Now *Herod*, the great cruel king, was not of the tribe of *Judah*, but an *Idumean*; therefore, the *Sceptre*, or kingly power, was, even in his time, beginning to move away from *Judah*. In his ſon's days, his kingdom was divided into four; and a *Heathen* governed the beſt of them, with the full and only power of putting evil doers to death. The *Sceptre* went further from *Judah* by this means, than before. And in lefs than forty years after CHRIST's death, *Jerufalem*, the whole Nation and Temple, were next to quite deftroyed. All this happened fome thoufand years after old *Jacob's* wonderful prophecy.

Q. 22. *How long did* John *continue to preach?*

A. Till JESUS was baptized, and came *in the power of the Spirit,* which he at his baptifm received, to qualify him for preaching his gofpel, and for confirming it by miracles.

Q. 23. *What became of* John?

A. He was caft into prifon, by *Herod the Tetrarch,* for reproving him; and foon after beheaded.

CATECHIST.

Let pupils read this affecting ftory, Mark vi. from verfe 14. Notice, firft, how terrible a thing an evil confcience is. Secondly, how hard an office it is, to be an honeft Minifter of religion. Thirdly, how cruel even a woman may become, if fhe once deliberately allow herfelf to commit any one grofs fin. Fourthly, how refpectable a thing *goodnefs* is, among the wicked themfelves. Fifthly, how dangerous a thing it is to get drunk. Sixthly, what an odds there is, between true and falfe honour, true and falfe religion. Finally, what praife and thanks is due to ALMIGHTY GOD, for being put under the inftruction of wife and good parents.

Q. 24. *Did* John *continue bearing witnefs for* JESUS, *till he died?*

A. Yes.

CATECHIST.

Here read two very pleasant passages. The first, in John iii. from verse 25. *Rabbi* signifies, master. The *Bridegroom* is, CHRIST. His *Friend*, *John*. Next, read Luke vii. 19, &c. Observe, that *John* well knew CHRIST before; but he would have his Disciples satisfy themselves, by something more than his own word. *John* was not like *a reed*, fickle and inconstant: he was not given to a soft and easy manner of life: he taught as a *Prophet*, and he foretold as a *Prophet*. The *kingdom of God* is the gospel; and it is of more advantage for any of us to live under this gospel, than to have been prophets before, if we improve our advantages as we ought.

Q. 25. *When* CHRIST *began to preach, was he followed by any number of disciples?*

A. Great multitudes followed him, and were astonished both at the wisdom of his words, and the might of his works.

CATECHIST.

Here read the beautiful heads of his discourse at *Nazareth*, Luke iv. from verse 16. and compare it with the ancient prophecy of *Isaiah*, which is there referred to, chap. lxi. from the begioning. A *Lecture* is explaining and improving a whole passage of Scripture. A *Sermon* is usually confined to a single text! The first of these is the most ancient, and best of the two. It has no less authority than that of CHRIST; and clearly condemns the too frequent practice of absenting Public Worship and Instruction, on the *Lord's* day forenoons. The *poorest* in station may, and ought, to understand CHRIST's doctrine. The *broken hearted* with trouble, and the sense of guilt, or sin, need CHRIST's doctrine much: likewise the *captives* or slaves of that shameful and dangerous thing: likewise, the

blind with ignorance: and finally, thofe who are *bruif-*
ed, as it were, with the *bondage* of meeting that death,
and judgement after death, which no one can efcape.
How *acceptable* fhould this *year*, or life be, in which fo
good a religion is preached unto us all ? But, if we do
not welcome it, the next *year*, or life, will be one of fore
and juft *vengeance*. *Gracious words* are, fweet and ufeful ones. The thing which fhould have led the people
of *Nazareth* to believe, was that which did foolifhly
and wickedly hinder them.   .

Q. 26. *Out of the number of thofe difciples,*
or followers, who were chofen to be the conftant
witneffes of his doctrine and miracles ?
A. Twelve.

CATECHIST.

See their names and their office fet forth, Matth. x.
from the beginning. *Unclean fpirits* are ufually accompanied with the fevereft bodily diforders ; fuch as
palfies, epilepfies, or the falling ficknefs, madneffes of e-
very degree and kind. The *Samaritans* were a mixed
people of *Jews* and *Heathens ;* and therefore, hated by
the *Jews*, more than even the *Heathens* themfelves.
What the *Apoftles* taught, was, in fubftance, what their
Mafter, and *John* before him, had taught. Their bufinefs, before the fufferings of CHRIST, required quick
difpatch : likewife generous love to others ; and con-
tentment with few outward conveniences.

Q. 27. *Did they travel with him through the*
feveral parts of the country of Judea ?
A. Yes; and were often with him at
Jerufalem, and in the time of the three
great yearly feafts of the *Jewifh nation.*

CATECHIST.

Thefe were, the *Paffover*, or feaft of *unleavened bread*, the *Penticoft and Tabernacles*. All of which young people fhould be taught the meaning of; as defigned to commemorate deliverance from *Egyptian bondage*; giving of the law from *Mount Sinai*; and dwelling in tents, while miraculoufly fubfifted through the wildernefs. To the firft of thefe, under the *gofpel*, anfwers the death of CHRIST, as the *Lamb of God*. To the fecond, the defcent of the *Holy Ghoft*, narrated Acts ii. from the beginning. Read and explain, *cloven*, to reprefent the number of languages, in which they would be able to teach. *Fiery*, as powerful and efficacious. The *Feaft of Tabernacles* is anfwered by our living in frail bodies, like *tabernacles*, or tents, eafily hurt and liable to fall into pieces, or perifh, every new moment. Compare 2 Cor. v. from the beginning.

Q. 28. *Did* CHRIST *and his* Apoftles *preach the doctrine of* repentance?

A. Yes; he came to call the very worft of finners; and to affure fuch, that, if they did repent, ALMIGHTY GOD would forgive them.

CATECHIST.

Caufe the young learner to read here, two fine examples, out of a great many. Matth. ix. from verfe 9. Luke vii. from verfe 36. The fpiritual pride of the *Pharifees* made them more backward to repent, than any other. Read, to this purpofe, the beautiful parable in Luke xviii. from verfe 9.

Q. 29. *Did he teach men how to become bleffed, or happy?*

A. Yes.

CATECHIST.

Direct young people to peruse often, and attentive-ly, Matth. v. 1——12. *Poor in spirit*, signifies the mo-dest and praying. *Mourners* for sin; and even those whom ALMIGHTY GOD, for wise reasons, is pleased to afflict. *Meek* under provocation: slow to anger, and ready to forgive. *Righteousness* may be justice here; and, to *hunger and thirst after it*, holds out a very strong desire. The *merciful*, who pity and relieve to the ut-most all who are in want. The *pure* hate every kind and degree of obscene thought, word, and deed. The *peace-maker* loves good order and harmony; and they are the *children of God*, whom he dearly loves. To *suffer* in a good cause, is glorious; and the best of all causes, is, for CHRIST and his religion. There are dif-ferent degrees of glory in Heaven. For such noble sufferers in their persons, or goods, or reputation, the highest degrees are laid up.

Q. 30. *Do the laws of* CHRIST JESUS, *reach to the* heart *of man, as well as to the go-vernment of his* outward conduct?

A. Yes.

CATECHIST.

Here, read with the young, Matth. v. from verse 21. *anger* is forbidden, as well as *murder*; because this leads to give *bad names*; then *blows*; and blows which very often end in death. *Unlawful love* is a great sin; so are minced *oaths* great crimes: likewise, the very desire of *revenge*. We must love the worst of people with pity and good will. We must sincerely pray for them. Read next, Matth. vi. from verse 1. *alms, fast-ing and prayers*, in order to be praised for them by men, is base *pride and hypocrisy*.

Q. 31. *Hath* CHRIST *taught his* scholars *how to pray?*
A. Yes.

CATECHIST.

Upon this subject, read together, Matth. vi. 9——
14. GOD, as a *Father*, made us, preserves us, and hath redeemed us. He is a *common father;* and we should ever be in a temper to pray for all his children. The *name of God*, is GOD himself. *Hallowed*, honoured by worship. The chief thing in his *kingdom* is, the gospel, which shews the *will of God*, and how to do it. *Angels* in Heaven do this *will* chearfully and constantly; and so ought we. *Bread*, the most necessary of all food, is here put for every outward blessing of life. They who sin, are debtors to *God's justice*, and deserve punishment. It is needless to pray for pardon, if we are not heartily disposed to pardon others. They who *forgive* not, seek, in effect, their own damnation. AL-MIGHTY GOD tempts none; and none can *tempt* us, without his leave. He can *deliver from all evil;* for his is the *kingdom, and the power, and the glory.* Unless the heart consents to every petition, we do not pray: so the word *amen* teaches; which imports, thus let it be.

Q. 32. *What, then, according to the prayer taught by our* blessed LORD, *ought to be our principal concern?*
A. The *kingdom of God, and his righteousness*, Matth. vi. 33. or, to enjoy Heaven, and, to be prepared for it.

Q. 33. *What next?*
A. The necessaries for this world, without being anxious for more.

Q. 34. *Will* a good heart, *and a* good life, *under the influence of* CHRIST's Word *and* Spirit, *certainly bring us to Heaven in the end?*

A. Yes.

CATECHIST.

To this purpofe, read with great care, Luke x. from verfe 38. Both fifters were good; but *Mary* feems to have been the graveft, and moft improved of the two. Read alfo, John v. 24. To *hear*, is, to obey. *God, even the Father Almighty*, fent CHRIST. *Death* eternal, or *condemnation*, is the deferved punifhment of fin. Great light is thrown upon thefe momentous fubjects, by John x. 27——31. To *hear* in this place, is, to underftand. To *follow*, is, to obey, and imitate. To be *known of Chrift*, is, to be loved of CHRIST; as, to be *known of the Father*, is, to be loved of him. Compare Pfalm i. 6. and not to be known of CHRIST, is, to be difowned by him, and fhut out of Heaven. See Matth. vii. 22. The *Father and Chrift* are of one mind, one *will*, one *affection?*

Q. 35. *After what manner did* CHRIST *teach thefe excellent laws, and motives to virtue?*

A. *Firft*, With great *authority*, Matth. vii. 29.

CATECHIST.

He had in him the power of one, whofe right it was to command. Compare Matth. v. 18, 20, 22, 28, 34, 39, 44. Matth. vi. and vii. chapters throughout.

A. *Second*, In a plain, familiar way, for moft part.

CATECHIST.

Let young people peruse, with attention, Luke vii. from verse 22. The *poor* were his most numerous attendants. Compare with this, 1 Cor. i. from verse 26. certain doctrines of the *Christian Religion*, the *Jews* were unable to bear at the beginning, James ii. 5. Matth. xi. 25. and therefore, these were taught by the LORD JESUS in *parables*; that is, by way of comparing spiritual and heavenly things, to outward and sensible objects. Some fine examples of this sort, are to be met with in the xiii. chap. of St. Matthew; and the easier kind of them, like that of the *sower*, may be read.

Q. 36. *How were the* multitude *affected by his Discourses?*

A. They *wondered* even to *astonishment.*

CATECHIST.

Lead the young people to peruse and understand the following beautiful examples, Luke iv. 22, 32. *Gracious* signifies both *sweet* and *merciful.* Matth. vii. 28. Even his *enemies* were convinced by them; as in John vii. from verse 45.

Q. 37. *Did he work many* miracles, *to confirm his doctrine?*

A. A great many, of different kinds, in an instant, by a word or touch, and in the most open manner. See Luke vii. from verse 21. Here ought CHRIST's words, John v. 36. to be attentively considered. Likewise John xv. 24.

Q. 38. *Were any other* proofs *given, during the course of his Ministry, to the truth of his* doctrine *and* mission?

A. He was, at different times, attefted by his *Father* from *Heaven.*

C A T E C H I S T.

Here explain John v. 37. by what did happen at *Chriſt's Baptiſm,* Matth iv. 17. At his *Transfiguration,* or moſt extraordinary change upon the mount, Matth. xvii. from the beginning. And, laſt of all, John xii. verſe 28, ſome little while before he ſuffered. Remark now, that *Chriſt was glorified,* or rather, *the name of God was glorified in him, by the miracles* which he wrought; and afterwards, by the aſtoniſhing things which happened, even while he hung upon the croſs. Enlarge a little upon the *ſupernatural darkneſs; the rending of the veil of the Temple; the earthquake.*

Q. 39. *Did* CHRIST *know things that were done out of human ſight, and foretell any future events ?*

A. He diſcovered a clear knowledge of the thoughts and deſigns of men ; and alſo, very often declared what ſhould happen to himſelf and his Apoſtles, his religion, and even to his enemies.

C A T E C H I S T.

Read Luke vi. from verſe 6: a *withered,* or palſied *hand,* and the *right,* or working one too. Their *watching* was malicious ; and could not be concealed from the great *miracle worker.* The author of ſuch power, was above all *poſitive inſtitutions ;* as are acts of neceſſity and mercy, in every age. See likewiſe, Luke v. from verſe 27. *Hypocrites* are moſt apt to cenſure. The parable of the *muſtard ſeed,* ſhews how the *goſpel* was to extend itſelf from ſmall beginnings, Matth. xiii. 31, 32. He often foretold his own laſt ſufferings, death, and refurrection; as in Matth. xvi. 21. John ii. from verfe 18. Alfo, thofe of his Apoftles, Matth. x. from verfe 16.   How his *enemies* were to be deftroyed, is prophefied of, with a moft wonderful particularity, in Matth. xxiv. throughout; compared with Luke xxi. from verfe 5. A few hints, at firft, upon both thefe, will be fufficient.

Q. 40. *Did the* Prophets, *under the* Old Teftament, *foretell the coming of* CHRIST, *and the nature of his kingdom?*
A. Yes.

CATECHIST.

At firft, in a very general and dark manner, as in Gen. iii. 15. Afterwards, ftill more and more clearly, as the age of the world increafed.   Put young people in mind of John v. 39. with a requeft to get that fingle verfe by heart.   Here recollect the promife to *Abraham*, Gen. xii. 3. The prediction of old *Jacob*, Gen. xlix. 10. That of *Mofes*, in Deut. xviii. 15. When they have leifure for it, the following ftriking paffages may be read, Pfalms ii, xxii, cx. Ifa. liii. Dan. vii. 13. ix. 25. Mic. v. 2. Mal. iii. 1. iv. 1. Yet thefe are no more than fpecimens.   Then how *John Baptift* pointed him out with his finger, John i. 29. All, together, confirming old *Zacharias'* defcription, from Luke i. 76, &c. The gradually brightening order of *prophecy* was very like to that of a dawning day.   The full *fpring* of it was, CHRIST.

Q. 41. *Did* JESUS CHRIST, *as other* prophets, *know things that were to come?*
A. Yes.

CATECHIST.

And to the above named examples, add, that moft

of his *parables* were prophetic. Moreover, that certain of these were understood by his enemies ; and that they used all possible to defeat, but without effect. Here, point out the signal pains they took to hinder his rising forth of the *sepulchre* or grave, Matth. xxvii. from verse 62. Their industry and zeal to oppose truth became of great service to support it. Compare Psalm vii. 14, 15. The evidences, or proofs for CHRIST's divine mission, and the truth of his religion, may, for some time, terminate in reviewing these arguments : observing only, farther, that there are certain of his predictions fulfilling every day ; which may be considered as a standing miracle in the church.

Of this sort are, first, the present state of the Jews, Luke xxi. 24. compared with Rom. xi. from verse 11. When they would not yield to various and suitable means for their conversion, the *Apostles*, and other teachers of the gospel, turned to the *gentile*, or heathen idolaters, to enlighten them ; and were amazingly successful. Next, some few and clear things may be noticed relative to the existence, progress, and downfal of the Romish Church, from 2 Thess. ii. throughout the greater part.

What greater *falling away*, or apostatizing from the simple truth of CHRIST, could well be, than to authorize *sin*, or to connive with it, by selling pardons for money ; and even indulgences to commit crimes afterwards ? Was not this *opposing and exalting himself above God ;* as well as above human law, *Judges and Magistrates, called.* likewise, *gods* in Scripture ? Was not this done *in the Temple,* or church of GOD ? Did not the *taking* heathen *Roman Emperors* out of the way, by the establishment of *Christianity* over all their empire, turn the heads of many both civil Rulers, and chief ecclesiastical ones ; and, by degrees, assume this frightful form ? Did they not pretend to vindicate their *Satanish lies*, by miraculous *powers and signs ?* And are they not *sinners*, or a *man of sin*, by a title of deserved infamy, who could spill such torrents of precious blood, in every stage of their corruption, the better to establish iniquity by law? Some plain and affecting instances should be singled out to tender minds, to impress them early with an aversion to cruel measures, even upon pretence of faith, or divine worship; and what a privilege it is, to enjoy sweet and useful freedom.

Q. 42. *How did* CHRIST *behave toward his* Disciples?

A. With the utmost *meekness* and *condescension.*

CATECHIST.

Explain *meekness*, by the words mild, soft or gentle. And, by way of example, let pupils read Mark iv. from verse 36. They had seen him work miracles, and knew that he could not be drowned; or, they might and ought to have done so, before he had finished his work. Even after Peter had denied him thrice, and the rest forsook him and fled, he calls them *brethren*, Matth. xxviii. 10. His rebuke is wonderful, John xxi. from verse 14. And his yielding to *Thomas* no less so, John xx. from verse 24. This explains *condescension;* as does the great pains he took to instruct two mistaken Disciples about the nature of his kingdom, Luke xxiv. from verse 13. How he looked upon *Peter* to convert him, *was both meek and condescending*, Luke xxii. 61.

Well might he say to them, as in Matth. xi. 29. Read. And well might the *Apostles* say, as in 2 Cor. x. 1. Read. The *hasty* and *passionate* should blush with confusion, and dread to abide in such culpable tempers.

Q. 43. *How did* CHRIST *behave toward his* enemies?

E

A. Such of them as were wilful and obflinate, he reproved with a bold and conflant fpirit.

CATECHIST.

Read a good part here of Matth. xxiii. from the beginning. *Mofes' Seat* fignifies as they read out of *Mofes' Law.* Their *heavy burdens* were moft of them contrived laws of their own. They had no Scripture authority for them; but pretended that they were cuftoms of their fathers. An example of the great danger of trufting to any thing in religion, but what is written. They affected a kind of *infallibility*, which, either in *Jews* or *Chriflians*, is vain and dangerous. *Hypocrites* may be fufpected from a great likenefs to the manners of ancient *Scribes* and *Pharifees;* but, to be fure of them, in every cafe, would require that we knew mens hearts, as CHRIST did; which belongs not to any.

Q. 44. *Who, among the* Jews, *were moft wilful and obflinate in their oppofition to* CHRIST?

A. The *chiefs* of their nation, both in church and ftate; particularly, indeed, the former.

CATECHIST.

Direct the young to John vii from verfe 45. How ftriking a contraft between the *Rulers* and their inferior *Officers!* Yet, they were not all alike bad. Read, likewife, John xi. from verfe 47. The *Priefts* and *Pharifees* own the *many miracles* performed by JESUS; and yet they take *council* againft him, that *he fhould die,* however much he had the countenance of the ALMIGHTY. No proofs can be more direct, of what a corrupt people, in the beft employments of life, will do.

Q. 45. *Did they continue his enemies to the laft?*

A. They could not reft, till he was put to death.

Q. 46. *What were the principal caufes of their hatred and cruelty?*

A. *Envy,* and the *love of this world.*

CATECHIST.

Remind pupils of examples under *Queft.* 34. and add thereunto *Pilate's* clear conviction of their unrighteoufnefs, Matth. xxvii. 13, 14. Luke xxiii. 4. Mark xv. 10.

Q. 47. *Did* CHRIST *know, before hand, the time of his departure out of this world?*

A. Yes, as appears from John xviii. 4. and he prepared himfelf for it.

Q. 48. *As how did he prepare himfelf?*

A. *Firft,* He took an affectionate leave of his Difciples.

CATECHIST.

Read with pupils, John xiii. 33. CHRIST was foon to die; but they were to live after him under trial, and would need each others beft help.

A. *Second,* He inftructed them how to be mutually ferviceable, John xiii. 34, 35. likewife, how to bear fo great a trial otherwife.

CATECHIST.

Here the xiv, xv, and xvi. chaps. of John fhould be much recommended; and the advantages of faith in divine affiftance, with the clear hope of a future and better world, fet before young minds.

A. *Third*, He inftituted a memorial of himfelf, and of his laft fevere fufferings.

CATECHIST.

Read Matth. xxvi. 26, 27. Mark xiv. 22, 23, 24. Luke xxii. 19, 20. Shew how much, in fubftance, they are the fame. *Taking bread, breaking and eating*, are natural actions ; as are, *taking the cup of wine, giving it to the difciples, and their drinking of it.* The fpiritual action, which went before each of them, was *bleffing God ;* or *giving thanks to him :* for fo the different accounts compared, do plainly reprefent that matter. The little word *it*, has no word in the original Greek to anfwer thereunto ; and the true tranflation of the whole in *St. Matthew*, is, *he bleffing*, viz. GOD ; not, *he bleffed.* Thofe actions, both natural and fpiritual, are explained, firft, by declaring, with relation to that performance, *this is my body which is given for you ; and this is my blood of the New Teftament, which is fhed for many, for the remiffion of fins :* or, *this is the New Teftament in my blood, which is fhed for you.* Secondly, by the command of it's divine Inftitutor, in thefe words ; *Take, eat ; and do this in remembrance of me.* The words *Teftament, and Covenant*, are of the fame import ; and hold out *the inftitution of Chrift's religion.* Compare 2 Cor. iii. 6. Heb. ix. 8, 15. Exod. xxiv. & xxxiv. 28. The *Jewifh inftitute* was the firft, and the *Old Covenant ;* and the *Chriftian* is called the *Second* or *New.* By *blood of the New Covenant*, and by *the New Covenant in that blood*, is meant the fame thing. So *the blood of flain beafts*, Exod. xxiv. 8. is called the *blood of that Covenant. Body and blood*, together, fignify death, 1 Cor. xi. 26, 27. and Rom. vii. 4. compared. This is the memorial, then, of CHRIST'S death, in confirmation of his *New Covenant ;* the fubftance whereof is, *repentance and remiffion of fins :* the one affured, by the awful *dying feal* of our *divine Saviour ;* and the other folemnly obliged to, by the fame *dying feal*, and this moft facred memorial of it. Nothing can more powerfully affect the confciences of men, than fuch an argument; and such is the use we are to make of this *eucharistical,* or *thanksgiving ordinance.* If any thing can prevail upon men, to be faithful in obeying the *new Covenant,* it must be *devoutly remembering* the terms, and privileges, as above set forth. As CHRIST is all in all to us; so the remembrance of him (whose history, under grace, works upon our minds by knowledge and consideration) is an excellent mean for promoting everlasting righteousness, and universal virtue: and giving it an establishment, sovereignty and empire, in our souls and lives. O ye young, be disposed thus to pray, "Suffer me never to forget him, who loved my " soul unto the death; and whose blood is the price " of my redemption: and let the remembrance of " what he has done and suffered for me, engage my " heart to love and serve him for ever."

N. B. The preparation for the whole was, our *blessed Lord's* observance of the *Jewish Passover* with his disciples. Read Luke xxii. 15, &c. After the close whereof, in which they were wont to *eat bread, and drink wine with thanksgiving,* he did apply that pious custom unto the *new Testament, Covenant,* or state of religion, to be set up in his death; and so some explain verse 18 Thus, as *baptism* was taken up from a like use of baptism among the *Jews,* so was the other. It was the same rite; but with a *new,* and infinitely more excellent appropriation, under the pure spiritual *kingdom of God* begun, and to be carried on while the world lasts, under the *great Messiah.* Blessed be GOD, that this most perfect state of religion is come! Let all whom it prevails upon to live religiously, come to his *holy Table,* and say; " I eat this in remembrance of " CHRIST; *and give thanks* to the name of his and our " *heavenly Father* for the *gospel Covenant;* and for the " sure hope of salvation by it's glorious Author. In " the same way, do I drink this, in remembrance of " his death. I commemorate an obligation, establish- " ed by the *blood of Jesus;* and renew the dedication " of myself, soul and body, to his service. *Amen.*

" Blefling, honour, and glory be unto the *moſt high*
" *God*, through Jesus Christ, who hath redeemed
" men of all nations of the earth, from fin and mifery,
" by his blood : and may our fincere celebration of
" both *Father* and *Son* here upon earth, be completed
" in the higheſt tranfports of thankfgiving, praife, and
" adoration in Heaven, for ever and ever." *Amen.*

A. *Fourth*, He retired; for prayer and meditation, into a private place.

CATECHIST.

Read with young and tender fouls, Luke xxii. from
verfe 39. He chofe to do this under cloud of night,
to prevent commotions. His compofure, throughout,
is aftonifhing ; *for he knew all things that ſhould come
upon him.* He might have drawn a veil over the whole
fcene ; but he was at an infinite diftance from diffimulation and difguife. To open up the heart to God,
by *prayer*, we muſt ſhut it up to men. Our moſt intimate Friends have a claim to ſhare in our deepeſt forrows. *Behold, and fee, if ever any forrow was like unto
this forrow!* Here is no ftoical feellefsnefs. *Good God!*
how affecting to fee the *divine Saviour* of the world,
and lover of fouls, in this extreme horror of mental
diftrefs ! What ought we not, as true believers in him,
to facrifice to it? How fubmiffively ſhould we bear
our heavieſt griefs? Even while *Omnipotence* afflicts,
he is to be invoked as a *Father*. Be ftill, and venerate the *unknown caufes* of a profufe and clotted *fweat,
like unto blood.* The moſt perfect characters may yet
be fimilarly tried; and fo great an example, they ſhould
be ambitious to imitate in the beſt manner poſſible.

Q. 49. *How was* Christ *found out by his
enemies, in that retirement ?*

A. He was betrayed into their hands by
Judas Iſcariot.

CATECHIST.

Read with pupils, Matth. xxvi. 14, 15, 16. The word *betray* fignifies, bringing any one into trouble, by an outward appearance of friendfhip. He made the firft fhocking propofal; and his bafe motive was, the *love of money*. His *proud wrath* alfo took offence, at a fair warning afterwards. Read likewife, Matth. xxvi. 47—50. and Luke xxii. 48. The mind of Jesus appears great, even to aftonifhment, by the manner in which he receives *Judas*. This was furely a moft affecting trial. It would appear, at the time, a fad prejudice to *our Saviour's* reputation. It would have funk or irritated any other to a great degree. But his reproof was *mild* and *piercing*.

Q. 50. Did Christ *attempt to relieve him-self?*

A. No; but he fhewed his enemies, that they could not lay hold of him without his own confent.

CATECHIST.

Read with the young, John xviii. from the beginning. A *brook* is a fmall rivulet, in common. That of *Cedron*, at the bottom of a deep glen, between the mount on which the Temple ftood, and that of *Olivet*. The fides of both were covered with trees and brufhwood: therefore, though it was full moon, they needed *Lanthorns*, &c. The enemies of Jesus fall to the ground, upon his uttering two words. Here he could have kept them; and when they were allowed to rife, he provided for the fafety of his yet fearful *Apoftles*. Then he yielded up himfelf. Compare, and enlarge upon the juftice and beauties of John x. 17, 18. with Phil. ii. from verfe 7. What great prefence of mind, and compofure of thought! He was innocent, and fpeaks out from confcious intregity; fo that, they

were ftruck as with lightning. Let us herein admire at once the dignity and condefcenfion of the
LORD JESUS. He is able to fave; and yet refigns
himfelf to fuffering, agreeable to the *Father's* will.

Q. 51. *Whither was he led?*
A. To the *chief Priefts* and council of
the Jewifh nation, who examined and con-
demned him.

CATECHIST.

Read John xviii. from verfe 13. *Caiaphas* was a man
of no confcience; as appears from John xi. 19, &c.
His queftion which he put to JESUS, John xviii. 19.
was quite unfair; and fhewed him to be very carelefs
about religion. CHRIST's reply is calm, meek, and
full of dignity. His words to the *officer* cannot be fuf-
ficiently admired. They hold out to us a great example of Matth. v. 39. As he had been tender of his
friends, fo he would not now facrifice to illegal ufage
any clear, juft human right. He would oblige accuf-
ers to direct themfelves by proof. Every one muft be
fenfible of this propriety.

Q. 52. *Was the* Jewifh *condemnation fuffici-*
ent to put CHRIST *to death?*
A. No: they accufed him and profecut-
ed him before *Pontius Pilate.*

CATECHIST.

Read John xviii. from verfe 28. Obferve, firft, the
Jewifh fuperftition; fecond, their rage; third, how
much better the *heathen Judge* did behave than they;
fourth, what a noble witnefs to the *Truth* CHRIST
was; and, laft of all, the pure and excellent nature
of his *kingdom.* He would not be liberated; read and
compare thofe highly inftructive paffages which follow:

John xviii. 10, 11. Matth. xxvi. 52—54. Luke xxii. 51, 52. He is apprehended as a *thief*, or other kind of infamous *malefactor*. Compare John xviii. 12. Matth. xxvi. 55, 56. Luke xxii. 52, 53. How sensible was our Lord's frame, and yet, how serene! How hard and obstinate the hearts of his enemies! Let us not neglect the earliest rebukes of conscience; but submit to admonition. If we enter into wrong designs, let us not persist in them. *Unrighteous Judges* may affect a regular procedure. See Matth. xxvi. 59——62. The silence of our Lord in midst of falsehoods, and unmerited outrages, was highly becoming. Yet there was a time to speak; and he nobly laid hold of it, Matth. xxvi. 63——66. "Thou hast said;" or, *It is as thou hast said.* My claim and character, hereafter, will be signally justified. *Truth and Courage* ennoble human nature. Being put upon oath, we must not hesitate to declare, from dread of personal consequences. A stranger misinformed is peculiarly pitiable, and soon to be set right. Mark the justice of *Paul's* observation, 1 Tim. vi. 13. The *partial* and *unequitable* have no such title; see and admire the lover of truth, Matth. xxvii. 12—14. Luke xxiii. 4——11. Conspicuous innocence, among such, is it's own noblest defence. Was it possible to work a reform, where *Barabbas* had the preference to one whom they could convict of no sin; and whose ministering had been so useful? Be astonished at the accounts given! Matth. xxvii. 16, &c. Mark xv. 7, &c. Luke xxiii. 25, &c. John xviii. 40. "Silence " here," says one most significantly, "was greater " than all words."

Q. 53. *Was he accordingly crucified?*
A. Yes; near *Jerusalem*, in the common place of execution, and between two thieves.

CATECHIST.

Read Luke xxiii. from verse 39. John xix. 13, 16.

The fentence is in few words, and could never warrant
the various unnatural and fhocking infults which followed upon it, Mark xv. 15——20. and compare, 1
Pet. ii. 23. He ufes no expoftulations nor complaints,
on his own account; and yet laments with deep diftrefs, the guilt, and impending miferies of the *Jewifh
nation.* Dwell in thought, upon Luke xxiii. 26, &c.
How excellent a temper! He would receive nothing
to ftupify his fenfe of pain, Mark xv. 22, 23. His deter-
mination was, to give a complete example of patience.
Forgivenefs keeps pace with generous *felf-denial,* Luke
xxiii. 32—34. when tortures were moft acute, the
prayer of compaffion is uttered; and it was a prayer
of *firm faith*, no lefs than *benevolence. Scoffs,* though
very trying, are meekly to be born; compare Matth.
xxvii. 39, 42, 43. Luke xxiii. 35, 36. Think now of
that beautiful fimilitude, in Ifa. liii. 7.

On the *Crofs,* our *bleffed Lord* hears and is moved
with the petition of a humble penitent, Luke xxiii. 43.
The great behaviour of Jesus under fuffering did, no
doubt, add to the probable faith and love which he had
before this. Affliction is fanctified, even to a great
finner. The *knowledge of Chrift* makes an entire convert of him. He profeffes belief, amidft numerous
and cruel enemies. He has refpect to a future *kingdom,*
and is approved. *Paradife* in that very hour, or *day,*
is with full authority promifed to him. How great is
Jesus here! He triumphs every where, fays one.
And how glorious is this triumph! To the laft, he
carries on, and accomplifhes his great defign of con-
verting and faving finners. Few apparent death-bed
penitents have fuch advantages, and attain fo high.
Under every divine teftimonial which accompanied
the crucifixion, the other thief hardens.

Q. 54. *Was any thing elfe worthy of peculiar
notice, faid or done by* Jesus, *while he hung upon the Crofs?*

A. Another very obfervable, towards his *mother Mary.*

CATECHIST.

Caufe the following fhort hiftory to be read, with leifure and great care, John xix. 25——27. It was for her honour, that fhe could be prefent at fo mournful a fcene; as it was for the honour of our *bleffed Lord*, that he took fuch notice of her. *Mary's* fortitude and zeal, like thofe of *John*, were noble. To *John*, the love of JESUS was peculiar, compare John xiii. 23. xxi. 20, 24. It was that of a *bofom friend.* Simple, and yet ref-pectful, was the addrefs of, *woman. Behold* one who fhall henceforth care for you, as if he were thy own dear *Son. Behold* her, whom, in all time coming, thou art to refpect and care for as thy own affectionate *Mother.* How amazing is this compofure, and filial re-gard! How blifsfully communicative is a fpirit of pure friendfhip! Such a legacy is, to the beft of all hu-man affections, a legacy of high honour and profit.

Q. 55. *What were the extraordinary things which happened during the crucifixion of* JESUS? A. *Firft,* Three hours darknefs.

CATECHIST.

See and compare Matth. xxvii. 45. Mark xv. 33. Luke xxiii. 44, 45. From the *fixth to the ninth*, accord-ing to the computation of thofe times, was, from twelve at noon till three afternoon. It might refemble that of a total eclipfe of the fun, in which there is light to a certain degree, and reached over all *Judea.* Being now *Paffover time* and full moon, the darknefs muft have been fupernatural. Very affecting, furely, where CHRIST had preached, and wrought fo many miracles, as a fign of Divine difpleafure!

A. *Second,* Rending the veil of the Temple.

CATECHIST.

See Matth. xxvii. 51. Mark xv. 38. Luke xxiii. 45. This veil did separate between the holy place, or the sanctuary, and the holy of holies, Heb. ix. 3. compare with this, the description of Exod. xxvi. 31—33. It was of the strongest contexture, as well as rich. There can be no doubt but many of the *Jewish Priests* must have seen this; which did foresignify the sudden destruction of the *Temple*, and speedy abolition of the rites of the *Mosaic Law*.

A. *Third*, An *Earthquake* at *Jerusalem*, but especially at *Mount Calvary*, where our *blessed Lord* was crucified.

CATECHIST.

See Matth. xxvii. 51. and how it was understood, verse 54. The effects of this extraordinary event are still to be discerned, in the *rock* which then rent.

A. *Fourth*, The opening of sepulchres or graves.

CATECHIST.

Read Matth. xxvii. 50—53. The *holy city* means *Jerusalem*, Matth. iv. 5. Luke iv. 9. By concussion from the *earthquake*, they might be thrown open. Compare Matth. xxvii. 58—60. John xix. 41. The *saints* do not appear to have been eminent ancient *patriarchs or prophets*, because of Acts xxiii. 25——31: but more probably good men, who had lately died; and who, upon going into *Jerusalem*, would be well known to their friends still living. *Saints*, in the *new Testament*, often denote disciples of JESUS, Acts ix. 13 ——32. compare chap. xxvi. 10. Rom. xv. 25, 26. They did not come out of their *graves*, till after CHRIST's resurrection; or early in the morning of that same first day of the week. Many friends and acquaintance, though poffibly, afterwards, to others. They might for a while, as *Lazarus* did, remain examples of modeft undiffembled piety. Some have thought, that to this important fact, John v. 25. might have a reference, by prophefy. Doubtlefs the miracle muft have been of great advantage to fome, to confirm their faith, and animate them under fubfequent trials and difficulties. The death of JESUS, even as his life had been, was full of wonders, and all beneficent. We owe to him, therefore, all honour and reverence. He is to be obeyed, in the face of every oppofition.

Q. 56. *What became of his dead body ?*

A. It was buried in a new *fepulchre*, or *grave.*

CATECHIST.

Read John xix. from verfe 38. *Jofeph* came with his fervants, *and took down the body.* It was *wound up* much as childrens are, foon after they are born. *Sepulchres* for the rich, were large enough to receive many dead bodies ; and the only entrance to them was, by the door ; being, for moft part, a *great ftone*, and not eafily removed. Compare Ifa. xxii. 16.

Q. 57. *How long did the body of* CHRIST *remain in the grave ?*

A. Three days, in the Jewifh way of fpeaking, or a part of them ; that is, from Friday afternoon, till early on the firft day of the week, now termed the *Lord's Day.*

Q. 58. *Why fo called ?*

A. Becaufe he then rofe, according to the Scriptures.

F

CATECHIST.

Read Acts ii. from verse 24. *Pains*, bands or cords of death. It *was not possible*, that he so holy, and every way acceptable to the *Father, should be holden* a close prisoner in the grave, compare John x. 17, 18. nor could his eternal truth, in prophesy, be contradicted. *David*, in spirit, *foresaw the Lord Christ*, and did speak of his *resurrection*. Compare Acts 13. from verse 33.

Q. 59. *Did* CHRIST *foretell his own rising again?*

A. Yes; and that often.

CATECHIST.

Lead pupils to compare Matth. xxvi. 61. with John ii. 18, *&c.* Hence it appears, that the *Jews* themselves understood his meaning; though they were much inclined to pervert his words. See, also, Matth. xii. from verse 38. chap. xxvii. from verse 62. Now did CHRIST's enemies, but without designing it, contribute to evince the truth.

Q. 60. *Of whom was he seen?*
A. Of the *Apostles*, and several others.

CATECHIST.

Read with young people, Matth. xxviii. from the beginning; likewise John xx. from the beginning. Observe, that none of all the four *Evangelists* give the precise order of CHRIST's appearances; because, each of them chose what particulars were most agreeable to their own taste, or situation. What seems most probable, is, first, that the women, upon seeing the stone, when they were at a little distance from the sepulchre, rolled away, agreed to send part of their number back to *Jerusalem*, for the sake of *Peter and John*; who came, and found the body to be removed, but saw not

Jesus. Second, that not being safe for them to continue there, for fear of the *Jews*, they returned, and left the women. Third, some part of these soon did, as *Peter and John* had done before them. Mean while, fourth, *Mary Magdalene*, an affectionate disciple, could not be brought away with them ; and the Lord rewarded her love with a view of him, before the rest. He next appeared to the other women, in their way home. They all met at *Jerusalem*, and informed the *Apostles*. Two of the Disciples, that same day, met with him, on their way to *Emmaus ;* as may be seen at large, Luke xxiv. In the evening he made himself known to all the Apostles. Probably *Peter* had a special visit by himself, to encourage his repentance, and preserve his afflicted soul from despair. Compare 1 Cor. xv. from the beginning, with Acts i. 3. ii. 32. xiii. 28, &c.

Q. 61. *Was he seen by them at leisure, and more than once ?*

A. Yes; and for forty days, at different times, they did touch his person, eat and drink with him.

C A T E C H I S T.

Peruse with care, John xx. 24——29. *Thomas*, upon the whole, was affectionate ; but still more so was his *Lord and Saviour*. Evidence, below that of sight, may be a sufficient ground of belief and action : and there is a peculiar blessedness annexed to such *obedient belief;* as it shews great love for truth, and desire of religious knowledge ; manifests a humble teachable temper ; and, necessarily, must reach to numerous principles. Peruse, likewise, Acts i. from the beginning. *Passion* denotes suffering, and includes death. What more *infallible* or convincing proofs could be, than seeing, speaking, handling, and bestowing such a promise as that of manifold miraculous gifts, so soon fulfilled afterwards ?

Q. 62. *Do not the* Jews *alledge, that the disciples of* Jesus *came by night, and stole the dead body away?*

A. They did then, and still continue, it is probable, to do.

C A T E C H I S T.

Read with your young, Matth. xxviii. 11—15. The preparations for Christ's rising out of the sepulchre were gradual. See what immediately goes before this passage. When the body was gone, the *guard*, undoubtedly, had no farther business at the *Sepulchre.* It would require time to recover from their consternation; and in that space, the *Apostles* and other disciples would have much discourse among themselves, about what had happened, and might relate them to several. Possibly the *soldiers*, who went *not to the chief priests, for shewing all the things that were done, would speak of them to others.* Compare Matth. xxviii. 11. Can we suppose, that the *Priests and Pharisees* were not at pains to examine where the *Apostles* had been all night? Their very seeming to neglect, and decry the imposture, is against them. How unlikely, that a *guard of Roman soldiers* should sleep upon duty? Discipline among them was extremely strict. Their attendance was not long. How can men say what is done, when they are not awake? The operation of robbing a *new tomb, hewn out of a rock, and a large stone laid at the door of it*, must have been with great noise. The burial clothes were not removed, Luke xxiv. 12. John xx. 1——8. but laid together with clear marks of leisure and composure. A clandestine removal would have answered no good purpose in the world. Such an offence could expect no support, either from God or from men. The *Disciples* themselves seem not to have expected the resurrection; compare Luke xxiv. 9—11. They were all thrown into a state of dejection and despondence. No punishment was inflicted upon any, for taking away the body.   Upon the whole, the teſtimony of the diſciples concerning CHRIST's reſurrection is true and credible; the *ſaying* among the *Jews*, falſe and exceeding improbable.

Q. 63. *After the ſpace of forty days from* JE-sus' *riſing, what did happen?*

A. He then ſpake to his *Apoſtles*, as in Matth. xxviii. 18, 19, 20. and renewed to them the promiſe of the *Holy Ghoſt.*

CATECHIST.

Read over that great and comprehenſive paſſage with care. *Creature*, put for *man. Preach* as my ambaſſadors, and under the efficacious influence of *divine power*, Acts i. 8. *In the name*, or belief of the *Father, &c. Baptiſm* was a rite adopted from the Jewiſh method of admitting proſelyted heathens into their worſhip; and fitly emblematical of ſubſequent pure lives. *Teaching* both by example and precept.   The way of life is now open to all, and it is but one.

Q. 64. *What followed next?*

A. He was parted from them who had been his conſtant attendants, and received into Heaven.

CATECHIST.

Read Mark xvi. 20, 21. Luke xxiv. 50, &c. Acts i. 9, &c. Here he had poured forth many prayers and tears.   Here he would be better ſeen, and without any interruption.   From this time forth, he obtained full poſſeſſion of the kingdom prepared for him by the *Father.*   Compare Heb. viii. 1, 2. ix. 24. 1 Pet. iii. 22. CHRIST, as chief *ſhepherd and Biſhop*, affectionately *bleſſed and prayed* for his immediate ſucceſſors, compare Lev. ix. 22.   Thus did the meetings for *divine wor-*

ſhip in the primitive church begin and end. **From** the excellent doctrine taught by CHRIST, his having all along been *mighty in deed*, as well as *word,* the ſignal teſtimonies which were given to him from Heaven, in the time of his miniſtry, and during the time of his crucifixion, and at his death, the reſurrection and aſcent, are gloriouſly conſiſtent.

Q. 65. *How was the vacancy made by the aḃ poſtaſy and death of* Judas *ſupplied?*

A. Through the addition of *Matthias,* to the eleven Apoſtles, by divine appointment.

C A T E C H I S T.

Read Acts i. 15, &c. It was an eſſential requiſite in an *Apoſtle,* to be a witneſs of CHRIST's reſurrection; and to have *companied* with the reſt during his miniſtry. No bad names are given to *Judas;* which is greatly in favour of thoſe whom, by tranſgreſſion, he left.

Q. 66. *When was the* Holy Ghoſt, *according to promiſe, beſtowed upon the* Apoſtles?

A. At the *Pentecoſt* next following the *Paſſover,* at which JESUS had been crucified.

C A T E C H I S T.

Read Acts ii. from the beginning. From this time, the *Apoſtles,* and the men who were with them, began to ſpeak with divers tongues, and were qualified to preach the *goſpel* to all nations. Beſides the ſtated inhabitants of *Jeruſalem,* there were, at this time, *Jews* and proſelytes of the *Jewiſh religion* from different and widely diſtant parts of the world: men of great zeal, underſtanding, and prudence, who, when they heard them ſpeak the *wonderful works of God,* in the languages of the ſeveral countries in which they reſided, were aḃ *mazed and marvelled.* *Peter with the eleven* informed them, how that matter came to pass ; and thus, in effect, did Jesus appear to an innumerable multitude. Consider well, Acts ii. 36, 37, 38, &c.

Q. 67 *What followed from this discourse, and these exhortations ?*

A. Many *gladly received the word, and were baptized,* Acts ii. 41. *Signs and wonders were also wrought among the people.* Compare Acts v. 12, 14.

Q. 68. *How did those vast multitudes live together ?*

A. In the greatest harmony.

CATECHIST.

See Acts iv. 34, 35. ii. 41, &c. They were *stedfast* to what the Apostles taught ; united in close *fellowship* with them : *brake bread* together at the *Lord's Table;* and were much given to *prayer.* They were most eminently charitable, chearful, and simple in their whole manners ; and were much in favour even with those who did not fully believe. By all which means, they contributed not a little to enlarge the *Christian church.*

Q. 69. *How did they manage their public benefactions, or alms ?*

A. By men of *good report,* as well as eminent gifts, who were chosen to this one thing.

CATECHIST.

Read with young people Acts vi. 1——9. Daily ministering to the poor, though a noble and pleasant service, would have obstructed the main preaching work of the *Apoftles* too much; efpecially, as the *word of God increafed the number of the Difciples.*

Q. 70. *Did the number of Difciples increafe beyond the bounds of* Jerufalem?

A. Befides the *great company* of believers there, in a fhort time, feveral churches of the faithful gathered throughout *Judea, Galilee,* and *Samaria.*

C A T E C H I S T.

Compare Acts ix. 31. viii. 14, &c. On thofe who believed were beftowed the gifts of the *Holy Ghoft,* by prayer, and laying on the hands of the *Apoftles.* Hence, *edification,* ingenuous refpect for ALMIGHTY GOD, and *comfort* to a high degree, did prevail.

Q. 71. *Were thefe* Apoftles *and* Believers *unnoticed by the* Jews *and others, who had crucified their* Mafter?

A. Far from it. Even in the beginning, and much more during the progrefs of their doctrine, they went through many fevere hardfhips and fufferings.

C A T E C H I S T.

Direct young people to read, by way of illuftration, Acts iv. from the beginning. How great was the combined force of violence from ignorant *people,* artful, malicious *priefts,* and unbelieving *Sadducees?* What a change in the *Apoftles,* from their late timorous and dejected behaviour? Now they are knowing, difcreet, intrepid. They glory in diftrefs, for CHRIST's fake. They infpire the like fentiments in others. They could not be brought to difown or conceal a teftimony of *divine truth.* As Jesus had foretold, *so they fit upon twelve thrones,* as it were, *judging the twelve tribes of Israel,* Matth. xix. 28. Luke xxii. 30. compared. Sad is the condition of a people, when their Rulers and Teachers practife themfelves, and recommend to others, falfehood, prevarication, and other wickednefs! An inordinate love of worldly gain, and prevalence of any bad principle in the heart, are of the moft dangerous confequence. Guard againft every temptation, in particular, to falfefy or lie. Admire and imitate *Apoftolical* diligence and zeal.

Q. 72. *Were any of the* leading Jews *converted to the* true Faith?

A. Yes; *Saul,* called alfo *Paul,* who had been of the fect of the *Pharifees,* and educated by *Gamaliel,* a celebrated *Jewifh doctor,* from being a warm and violent oppofer and perfecutor of the Difciples of Jesus, was converted to the fame *faith,* by an extraordinary appearance.

CATECHIST.

Read an account of this, Acts ix. throughout; and compare, afterwards, chap. xxii. He received, immediately upon the back of this, the full knowledge of the doctrine of the gofpel by fpecial revelation; and was appointed an *Apoftle,* by Jesus Christ himfelf. See Gal. i. 1—12. Eph. iii. 3. As the other *Apoftles* had done, he alfo fpoke with tongues, wrought miracles in great variety and abundance, and conferred gifts of the *Holy Ghoft* upon his converts. By him, in company with *Barnabas,* the *gofpel* was boldly taught both to *Jews and Gentiles.* Obferve, by way of example, Acts xiii. 16 ——41. Likewife chap. xvii. 16——32.

Q. 73. *Was his success in particular very remarkable?*

A. It was indeed: for, having strenuously asserted the acceptance of the *gentiles*, and their right to all the privileges of the church and people of GOD, without the observation of the rites of the law of *Moses*, he formed congregations of *Christians* in many places from among the most ignorant and vicious idolaters.

CATECHIST.

Lead young people to understand how these societies were formed. Each person in them was, first, baptized, Acts ii. 41. viii. 12. Rom. vi. 3. 1 Cor. i. 13—16. then, they met together, and worshipped ALMIGHTY GOD, by *prayers and praises*, compare Gal. i. 2. 1 Cor. xiv. 33. xvi. 19. 2 Cor. viii. Acts i. 14, 24. ii. 42. vi. 4. 1 Cor. xiv. 14——17. They had discourses, likewise, and exhortations, and readings of the sacred writings, 1 Cor. xiv. throughout, Acts xviii. 11. xx. 7. Gal. vi. 6. Heb. xiii. 7. Col. iv. 16. 1 Thess. v. 27. As said before, they celebrated the memory of the death of JESUS CHRIST, by eating together bread, and drinking wine in a solemn manner, Acts ii. 42. xx. 7. 1 Cor. xi. 23.

Q. 74. *Upon what day of the week did the* primitive Christians *ordinarily meet for* religious worship?

A. Upon the *first*, called the *Lord's Day*, in memory of the resurrection of JESUS from the dead, Acts xx. 7.

Q. 75. *How did they behave themselves toward* Kings *and* Governors?

A. They were directed by the *Apostles* to pray for them ; and otherwise to behave in the moſt prudent, quiet and orderly manner, 1 Tim. ii. 1, 2. 1 Pet. ii. 13———18.

Q. 76. *Did the* LORD JESUS *favour thoſe ſolemn meetings ?*

A. Yes, by his ſpecial preſence, Rev. i. 10. and giving them the high pleaſure of contributing to the relief of their neceſſitous brethren, 1 Cor. xvi. 2.

Q. 77. *By whom were they conducted ?*

A. By *Miniſters*, called *Biſhops*, or *Elders*, or *Paſtors*, or *Teachers*, and *Deacons*.

CATECHIST.

Direct the young how to conceive of this decent and orderly manner for inſtruction in the principles and practice of piety, from 1 Cor. xiv. 32. Gal vi. 3. 1 Theſſ. v. 12. Phil. i. 1. Likewiſe, that the neceſſities of each member might be duly provided for, Acts xx. 28, with 1 Pet. v. 1, and the Epiſtles to *Timothy* and *Titus* may be recommended to private peruſal.

Q. 78. *From what claſs of men were theſe officers of the church choſen ?*

A. From thoſe who had been before approved, as perſons of integrity and capacity for the work to which they were appointed, 1 Tim. iii. 10. Acts vi. 2.

Q. 79. *Beſides teaching, and making a prudent and faithful diſtribution of the ſtock of the ſociety, was any thing elſe expected from them ?*

A. That they fhould be examples of all virtue to the reft of the *Chriftian Societies*, in which they prefided and miniftered; as thefe *Societies* themfelves were to be examples to the world around them, Matth. v. 13—16. Read.

Q. 80. *Did the Apoftles of* CHRIST, *together with their companions and fellow-labourers, evangelifts and others, leave the world much reformed?*

A. Before this, they had erected Societies or Churches of *Chriftians*, in moft parts of the *Roman Empire;* even the largeft and moft civilized countries and cities.

Q. 81. *Doth this Church of* CHRIST *ftill fubfift?*

A. It doth; and, according to his exprefs affurance, ever will, Matth. xvi. 16.

CATECHIST.

See, for the foundation, Eph. ii. 19, &c. Explain the *gates of Hell*, by the oppofition of adverfe powers, even to tortures and deaths of the cruelleft kinds.

FINIS.